Specials!

Rivers:
from source to sea

Mary Green

Acknowledgements

© 2007 Folens Limited, on behalf of the author.

United Kingdom: Folens Publishers, Apex Business Centre, Boscombe Road, Dunstable, LU5 4RL.
Email: folens@folens.com

Ireland: Folens Publishers, Greenhills Road, Tallaght, Dublin 24.
Email: info@folens.ie

Poland: JUKA, ul. Renesansowa 38, Warsaw 01-905

Editor: Saskia Gwinn   Layout artist: Book Matrix   Illustrations: Tony Randell
Cover design: Holbrook   Cover image: Corbis

'River Tale' by Mary Green first published in Ye New Spell Book, Macmillan 2002. Chosen by Brian Moses.

First published 2007 by Folens Limited.

Every effort has been made to contact copyright holders of material used in this publication. If any copyright holder has been overlooked, we should be pleased to make any necessary arrangements.

British Library Cataloguing in Publication Data. A catalogue record for this publication is available from the British Library.

ISBN 978 1 85008 187 6

Contents

Introduction   4

Water and the water cycle   5
Water in the environment   6
Where is water stored?   7
The water cycle   8
Water cycle keywords   9
Explaining the cycle   10

The course of the river   11
The river in the mountains   12
The river on the plain   13
The river meets the sea   14
River fact file   15
River Tale   16

River erosion   17
River erosion (1)   18
River erosion (2)   19
True or false?   20
What is weathering?   21
Erosion and weathering   22

River transportation   23
River transportation (1)   24
River transportation (2)   25
Cause and effect   26
What could happen?   27
What did happen?   28

River deposition   29
Meandering rivers   30
What is missing?   31
Oxbow lakes   32
An oxbow lake: how could one form?   33
River map   34

**River landscapes, drainage basins
and river valleys**   35
River valley   36
Drainage basins   37
How does a waterfall form?   38
The changing valley   39
Great rivers   40

Flooding   41
Overflowing rivers   42
What is happening?   43
Flood report   44
Bangladesh   45
Disasters and benefits   46

Floods: causes and control   47
Rivers and their floodplains   48
Case study: the River Lee   49
Why did the River Lee flood?   50
Soft and hard flood defences   51
Key points   52

River pollution   53
Dirty waters   54
Water quality   55
Case study: the River Ely   56
The River Ely: Looking more closely   57
River pollution summary   58

River conservation and renewal   59
Restoring a river (1)   60
Restoring a river (2)   61
The Los Angeles River   62
River file   63

Assessment sheet   64

Introduction

Specials! Geography is divided into ten units. A unit has one or more photocopiable resource sheets and several activity sheets. This allows the teacher to work in different ways. For example, the unit could be taught as a lesson with students in groups of varying sizes. Alternatively, a single resource sheet and its related activity sheets could be used as support material. The Teacher's notes give guidance and are laid out as follows:

Objectives
These are the main skills or knowledge to be learned.

Prior knowledge
This refers to the minimum skills or knowledge required by the students to complete the tasks. As a rule, students should have a reading comprehension age of 7 to 9 years and should be working at levels 1 to 3. Some student pages are more challenging than others and you will need to select accordingly.

QCA and NC links, Scottish attainment targets, Northern Ireland and Welsh links
All units link to the QCA scheme of work, the NC for Geography at key stage 3 and the Scottish attainment targets. Where relevant, there are also links to the programmes of study in Northern Ireland and Wales.

Background
This gives additional information for the teacher, expanding on geographical and historical details or giving further information about this unit.

Starter activity
Since the units can be taught as a lesson, a warm-up activity, focusing on an aspect of the unit, is suggested.

Resource sheets and Activity sheets
The resource sheet, which is often visual, but may also be written, does not usually include tasks and can be used as a stimulus for discussion. Related tasks are provided on activity sheets. Where necessary, keywords are included on the student pages. Other keywords are included within the Teacher's notes. These can be introduced to students at the teacher's discretion and depending on the students' ability.

Plenary
The teacher can use the suggestions here to recap on the main points covered or to reinforce a particular idea. Work related to assessment, ICT or other media may also be suggested.

Assessment sheet
At the end of each unit, students can use the assessment sheet to assess their own progress. The teacher should add a simple checklist of between three and seven points relating to the geography curriculum covered in each unit. Students can subsequently set targets to achieve according to their performance.

Other books in this series
Specials! Geography – **Physical processes**
Specials! Geography – **Local and world communities**
Specials! Geography – **Global issues**
Specials! Geography – **Mapping skills**
Specials! Geography – **Sustainable development**

Teacher's notes

Water and the water cycle

Objectives

- Understand how water is stored in the environment
- Understand the water cycle and the constant movement of water
- Learn the keywords: evaporation, transpiration, condensation, precipitation and infiltration

Prior knowledge

Students should be aware of water around them, particularly in its natural environment.

QCA links

Unit 7 Rivers – a fieldwork approach

NC links

Breadth of study 6 Themes c

Scottish attainment targets

Environmental Studies – Society – people and place
Strand – The physical environment
Level E

Environmental Studies – Science – Earth and space
Level F

Wales NC Links

Themes 2 Rivers or Coasts

Northern Ireland NC links

Weather and climate d

Background

Water covers almost two thirds of the planet and most of it is found in the seas and oceans. The remaining freshwater is frozen in glaciers and great ice sheets and is also found in rivers, streams, lakes, wetlands, in the ground as groundwater, in the atmosphere and, of course, in reservoirs. The perpetual movement of water is illustrated by the hydrological (water) cycle, which moves between the atmosphere, the land and underground. Water then finds its way into rivers from rain and other forms of precipitation and through run-off from the land. Some rivers will pass into lakes. Others will meet marshes or wetlands but most will flow into the sea. All these features, along with trees and plants, play their part in the hydrological cycle.

Starter activity

Discuss the keyword **reservoir** with students, noting the difference between artificial reservoirs where water is stored and the scientific term used to refer to the way water is stored in the natural environment, for example, seas and oceans, which are part of the water cycle. Ask students to identify as many places as they can where water occurs in the environment.

Resource and activity sheets

Take students through the resource sheet 'Water in the environment', comparing the comments they made in the Starter activity with the examples given of where water is stored. Ask students to identify the different types of water, for example, fresh water and salt water, and where these are found. Ask them to think about where most water is found (see **Background** for further information), where water occurs naturally and where it is stored artificially. Students should then complete the activity sheet 'Where is water stored?' on their own where they should use the writing frame provided to record what they have learned. When they have finished, ask students to read their statements to the rest of the class. Compare the differences in the students' statements.

The resource sheet 'The water cycle' should be used in conjunction with the two activity sheets, 'Water cycle keywords' and 'Explaining the cycle', and as far as possible should be used together in the same session. 'The Water cycle' resource sheet shows the main components of the water cycle (evaporation, condensation and precipitation). It also gives information on transpiration and infiltration, which teachers may wish to deal with at a later date. The keywords dealt with in this unit often prove difficult for students to recall and 'Water cycle keywords' provides syllables for each as a memory prompt. Talk students through the water cycle processes and in pairs ask them to explain each one to their partners. Ensure students can recall the water cycle processes provided on this sheet before asking them to complete the final activity sheet, 'Explaining the cycle', a writing fame which students should use to explain the water cycle with the help of keywords.

Plenary

Reinforce the water cycle keywords and the water cycle processes. Ask students to cut out and paste the keywords and their syllables into a word bank or spelling book.

Water in the environment

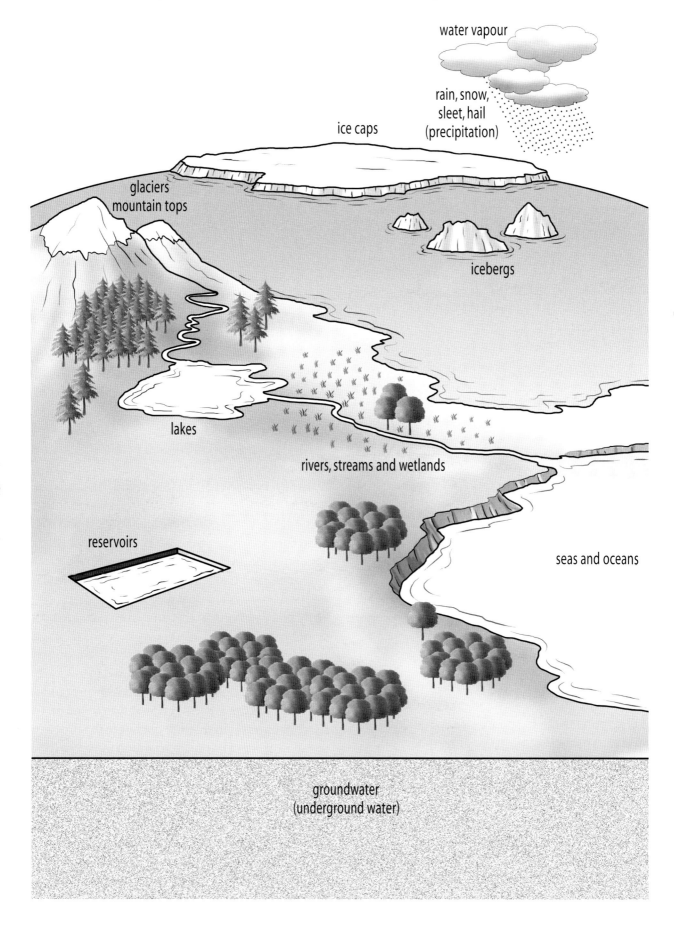

Activity sheet – Water and the water cycle

Where is water stored?

☞ Complete this writing frame to show how water is stored. You will need to use the resource sheet 'Water in the environment' to help you.

We have been finding out about…

....

I learned that…

....

and also…

....

Some…

....

While some...

....

and also

....

Most…

....

Resource sheet – Water and the water cycle

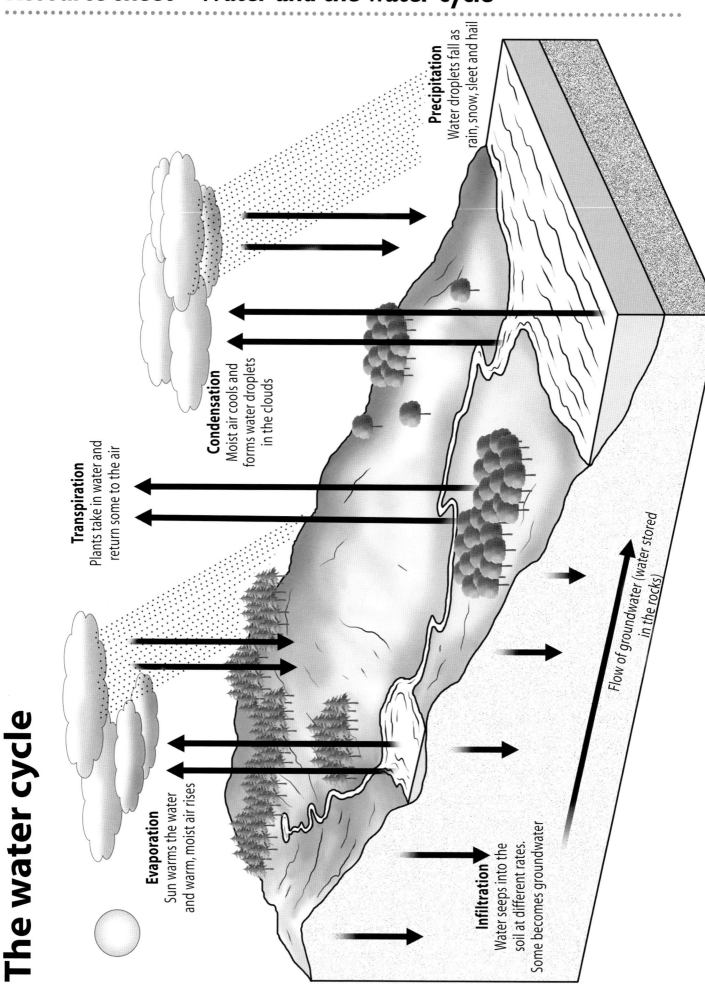

The water cycle

Precipitation
Water droplets fall as rain, snow, sleet and hail

Condensation
Moist air cools and forms water droplets in the clouds

Transpiration
Plants take in water and return some to the air

Evaporation
Sun warms the water and warm, moist air rises

Infiltration
Water seeps into the soil at different rates. Some becomes groundwater

Flow of groundwater (water stored in the rocks)

Geography Rivers: from source to sea

Water cycle keywords

☞ You will need to use this sheet with resource sheet 'The water cycle'. Match these words to their meanings. The first one has been done for you.

Words and syllables	Meanings
evaporation (e-vap-or-a-tion)	Plants take in water and return some to the air.
condensation (con-dens-a-tion)	The sun warms the water on land, seas, lakes, rivers and other places where it is stored. The warm, moist air rises.
precipitation (pre-cip-i-ta-tion)	Some water seeps into the soil at different rates. This depends on how porous the ground is. Some will become deep groundwater.
transpiration (trans-pir-a-tion)	Droplets of water fall as rain, snow, sleet or hail.
Infiltration (in-fil-tra-tion)	The warm moist air cools to form droplets of water.

Activity sheet – Water and the water cycle

Explaining the cycle

☞ Using the keywords below, explain the main points of the water cycle to a partner. Make some notes in this diagram first. It has already been started for you.

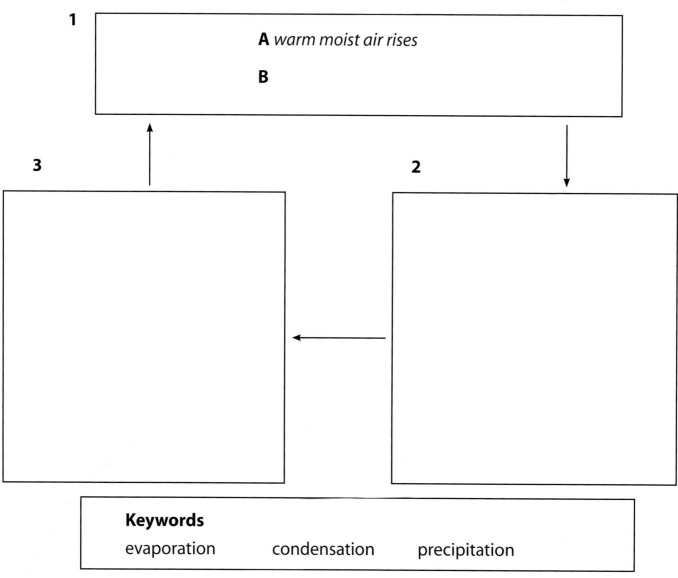

1

A *warm moist air rises*

B

3

2

Keywords

evaporation   condensation   precipitation

☞ Work with a partner and take it in turns to answer these questions.

In your partners, what is infiltration? What part does it play in the water cycle?

_____

_____

What is transpiration? What part does it play in the water cycle?

_____

_____

Teacher's notes

The course of the river

Objectives

- Understand the different parts of the river's course: upper, middle and lower
- Understand the keywords linked to the river's course
- Assemble a fact file using ICT

Prior knowledge

Students should be aware that a river changes from source to mouth.

QCA links

Unit 7 Rivers – a fieldwork approach

NC links

Breadth of study 6 Themes c

Scottish attainment targets

Environmental Studies – Society – people and place
Strand – The physical environment
Level E

Environmental Studies – Society – enquiry
Strand – Carrying out tasks
Level D

Wales NC links

Themes 2 Rivers or Coasts

Northern Ireland NC links

Rocks and processes of landscape development d
Fluvial

Background

Some rivers start as water from springs in the mountainside and converge to form a channel, while others may start as melting water from glaciers or begin their journey from lakes. When it is full with strong currents, it is very powerful. Once the river has reached its floodplain, it is much wider and deeper. By the time it approaches the sea (sometimes meandering in broad loops across the landscape), it has lost most of its power.

Starter activity

Ask students what they know about the river's journey and whether they have any concept of its divisions between upper, middle and lower course. Ask them if they are aware of any local rivers that feed into a principal river. For example, many tributaries feed into the Thames, such as the Cherwell, Thame, Lodden and Wey.

Show the students a page of classified adverts from a local or national newspaper. Have the adverts been sorted in any way? Can the students spot the patterns? Help them to understand that being able to organise things into different categories is a useful skill.

Resource and activity sheets

The resource sheets, 'The river in the mountains', 'The river on the plain' and 'The river meets the sea', deal separately with each part of the river's course. These resource sheets can be joined together (and laminated) to form the whole course of a river. Go through each resource page with students, highlighting the following keypoints: in the upper course, water may come from groundwater spilling on to the surface as streams; in the middle course, when tributaries join the main river, the volume of water increases. In the lower course, the river starts to travel more widely across its floodplain, creating meanders that become wider until it meets the sea. Once students understand the river's route, introduce the keywords as shown on the resource sheet, which track the course of the river. Ask selected students to explain the river's journey using the keywords as prompts.

The activity sheet, 'River fact file' can be used by students to gather information about some chosen rivers in the British Isles, which should not be local rivers, nor those mentioned in the units on flooding and floods: causes and control). Students should research this activity using the Internet and ICT with teacher guidance. This activity can also be used as a starting point to carry out a project on a local river section (see the unit on River conservation and renewal), using OS maps and undertaking fieldwork.

Read the poem, 'River Tale' to students. Discuss it in relation to the work carried out in this unit. Students may also wish to draw from their own general knowledge and experience with rivers.

Plenary

Ask students (or selected students) to give a short presentation, which should take only one to two minutes, on their chosen rivers. They should refer to their River fact files to help them.

The river in the mountains

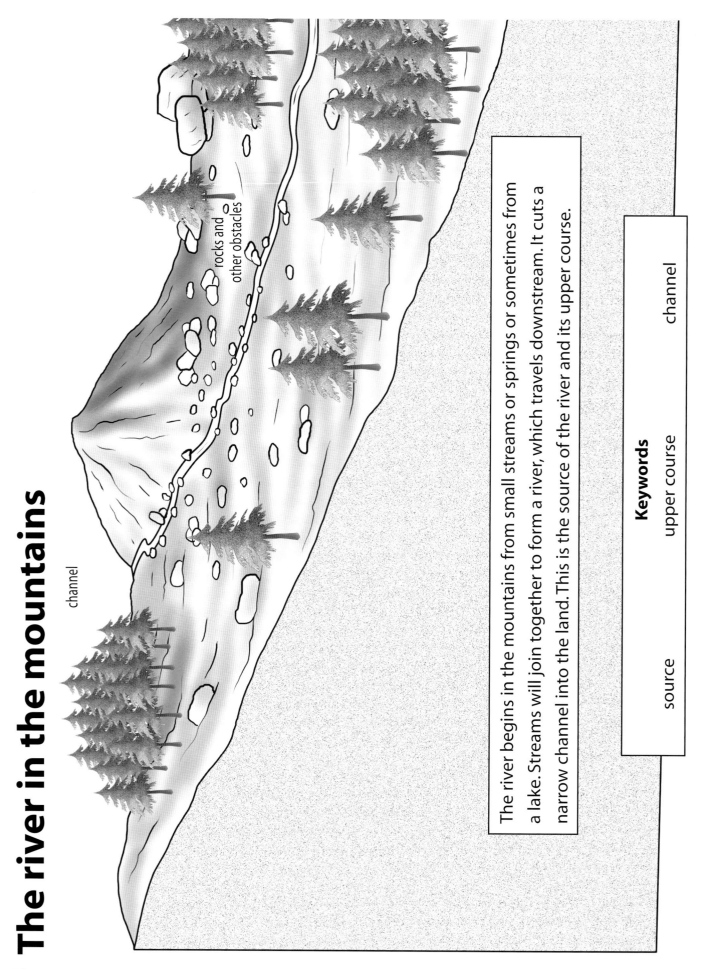

channel

rocks and other obstacles

The river begins in the mountains from small streams or springs or sometimes from a lake. Streams will join together to form a river, which travels downstream. It cuts a narrow channel into the land. This is the source of the river and its upper course.

Keywords

source   upper course   channel

Resource sheet – The course of the river

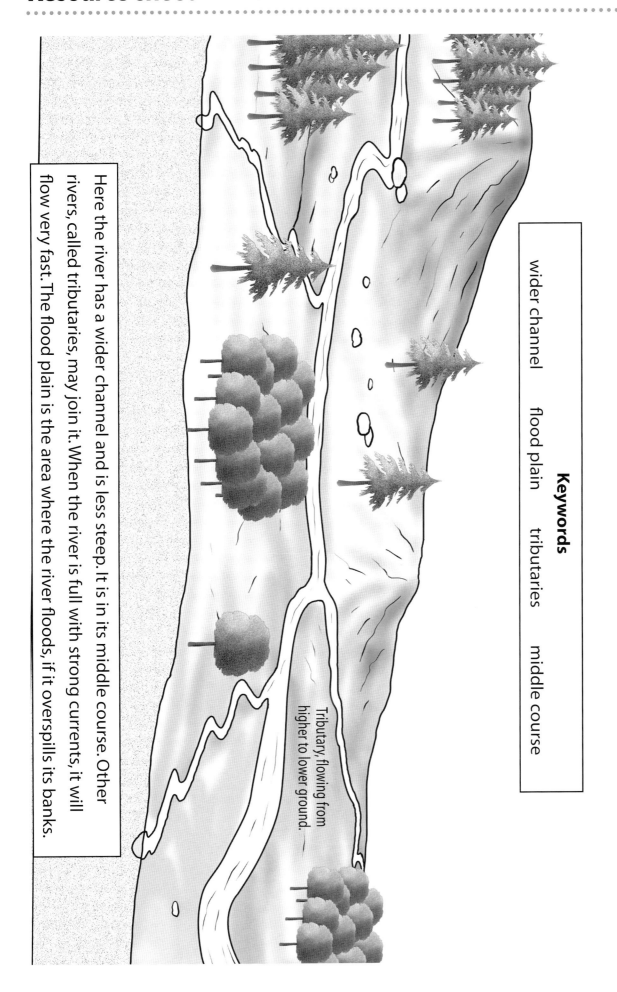

The river on the plain

Keywords

wider channel   flood plain   tributaries   middle course

Tributary, flowing from higher to lower ground.

Here the river has a wider channel and is less steep. It is in its middle course. Other rivers, called tributaries, may join it. When the river is full with strong currents, it will flow very fast. The flood plain is the area where the river floods, if it overspills its banks.

The river meets the sea

The river is now flowing much more slowly and has lost much of its power. It is in its lower course and can form wide loops across its flood plain. These are called meanders. It enters the sea at its mouth.

Keywords

meanders   mouth   lower course

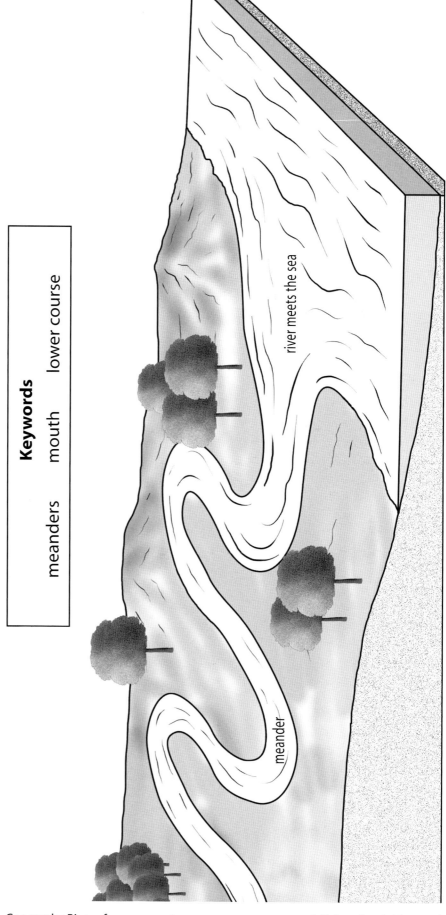

river meets the sea

meander

Geography Rivers: from source to sea

Activity sheet – The course of the river

River fact file

☞ Choose a river in the British Isles and find out about it. Use the Internet and ICT with guidance from your teacher to help you. Then, complete the fact file below.

Fact file
Is it a main river? **yes/no**
If 'yes' what are its tributaries?
If 'no', what river does it feed into?
Where is its source?
Where is its mouth?

☞ Now, write a paragraph about your river using this writing frame. Include:

- river crossings
- leisure activities
- wildlife

The river (name):

....

People….

....

And there is…..

....

For example……

....

River Tale

First gather morning rain,
Splash down mountainside,
Tip into rivulets, into tributaries and
Make a river.

Chase downstream fearlessly,
Catch cataracts,
Track eddies, spy leaping fish, then
Subside, yawning.

Now, trail wet toes carelessly,
Take detours,
Flow over floodplain, ripple in the sun,
Linger sleepily

And wait to hear
The lap of water shift across sand,
Crabs scuttle,
The moon spill out of the sea,
Curlews call,
And the river pass from source to estuary.

Mary Green

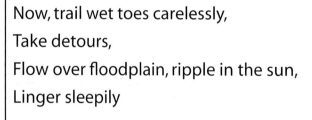

Geography Rivers: from source to sea   © Folens (copiable page)

Teacher's notes

River erosion

Objectives

- Learn how the river erodes by corrasion, attrition, corrosion and hydraulic action
- Understand the difference between erosion and weathering

Prior knowledge

Students should be aware that a river changes from source to mouth and understand the different courses of the river. They should be able to read some polysyllabic words.

QCA links

Unit 7 Rivers – a fieldwork approach

NC links

Breadth of study 6 Themes c

Scottish attainment targets

Environmental Studies – Society – people and place
Strand – The physical environment
Level E, Level D
Strand – Human-physical interactions
Level E

Wales NC links

Themes 2 Rivers or Coasts

Northern Ireland NC links

Rocks and processes of landscape development c, d Fluvial

Background

Erosion is the wearing away of materials by different elements such as water. Gravity can also cause erosion, with, for example, the movement of rocks and soil down a bank. Erosion is distinct from weathering, which occurs as rocks and soil breakdown naturally through different processes: physical (such as the action of weather), biological (such as the effect of plant roots) or chemical processes (such as acid rain). The important difference between erosion and weathering is that the latter has its effect in one spot, while the former (physical) shifts material from one place to another. River (and sea) erosion is caused by the continual movement of water over soil, rocks and other materials, which are carried in the water. In this way the landscape is changed, for example, the river bed and banks are created.

Starter activity

Describe an example of weathering to students such as the effect of acid in rainwater on gravestones. (If there are nearby examples, students could be shown these.) Ask them what they think is happening, ensuring that they grasp that the effect is a chemical reaction.

Resource and activity sheets

The two resource pages, 'River erosion 1 and 2' deal respectively with corrasion and attrition and corrosion and hydraulic action. You may wish to tackle these sheets together or separately. Go through the different river erosion processes with students, ensuring they grasp how each works. Refer to the keywords provided as needed. Emphasise to students that the river's energy causes erosion.

Follow the resource sheets with the activity sheet, 'True or false?', in which students must decide whether or not certain statements about river erosion are true or false. Discuss each statement with students as a class.

The last two activity sheets should be used together to study the difference between weathering and erosion. 'What is weathering?' looks at different types of weathering. Four pictures have been provided to show the different kinds of weathering. Students should study these with a partner and discuss what is happening in each, before separately writing down the answer to each. You may wish to explain to students the action of freezing water, which thaws, refreezes and so on, causing rocks to break down. Ensure children grasp that the car in figure 1 is rusty.

Once students have grasped what types of weathering are depicted, for example, 1 - chemical, 2 - biological, 3 - biological and 4 – physical, spend some time discussing the difference between weathering and erosion with students before instructing them to tackle the final activity sheet, 'Erosion and weathering', which they should complete on their own. A writing frame has been provided for students to complete.

Plenary

Check the keywords used in this unit, with students by asking them to record in a spelling bank all those that cause particular difficulty. Ensure students have grasped the different processes they have been studying. Finally, ask them to think of further examples of weathering in the environment around them.

Resource sheet – River erosion

River erosion (1)

☞ Rivers can wear away (erode) rocks and other materials in different ways. Study the pictures below. Make sure you know the meanings of the keywords.

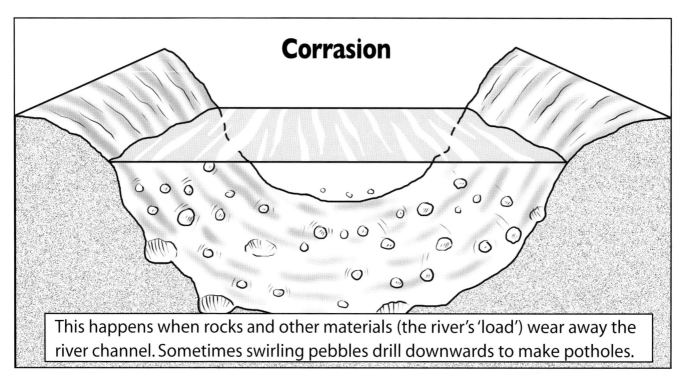

Corrasion

This happens when rocks and other materials (the river's 'load') wear away the river channel. Sometimes swirling pebbles drill downwards to make potholes.

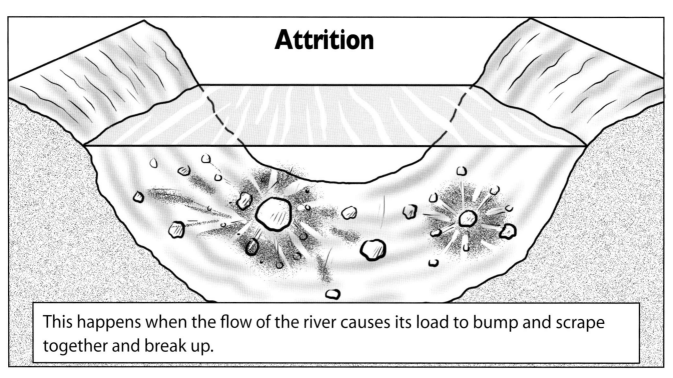

Attrition

This happens when the flow of the river causes its load to bump and scrape together and break up.

Keywords			
erosion	the river's load	corrosion	attrition

River erosion (2)

☞ Rivers can wear away (erode) rocks and other materials in different ways. Study the pictures below. Make sure you know the meanings of the keywords.

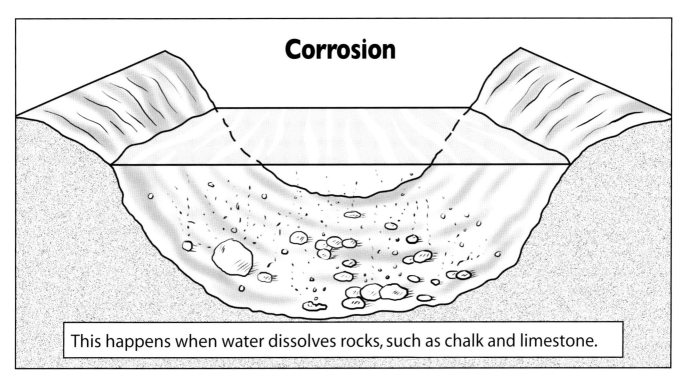

Corrosion

This happens when water dissolves rocks, such as chalk and limestone.

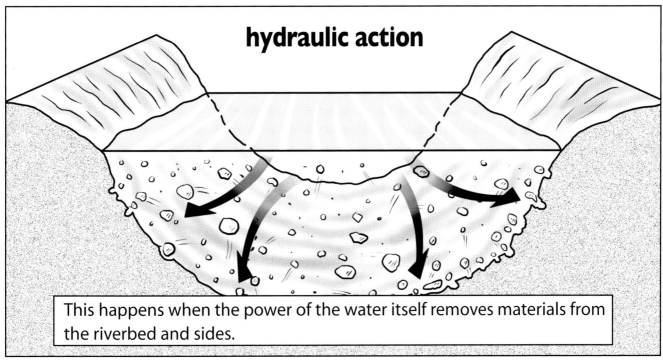

hydraulic action

This happens when the power of the water itself removes materials from the riverbed and sides.

Keywords		
corrosion	dissolve	hydraulic action

Activity sheet – River erosion

True or false?

☞ Tick true or false by each of these statements. Use resource sheets, 'River erosion (1) and (2)' to help you.

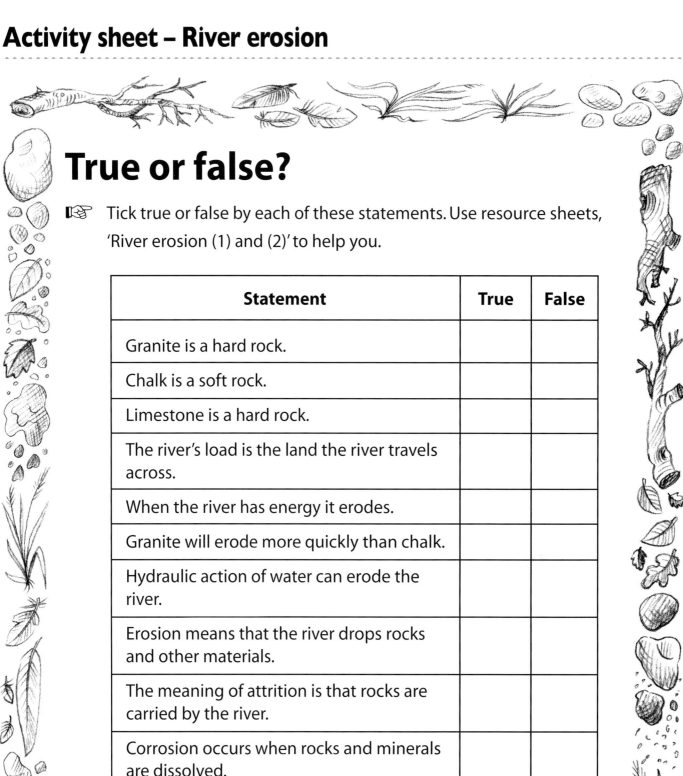

Statement	True	False
Granite is a hard rock.		
Chalk is a soft rock.		
Limestone is a hard rock.		
The river's load is the land the river travels across.		
When the river has energy it erodes.		
Granite will erode more quickly than chalk.		
Hydraulic action of water can erode the river.		
Erosion means that the river drops rocks and other materials.		
The meaning of attrition is that rocks are carried by the river.		
Corrosion occurs when rocks and minerals are dissolved.		
Corrasion occurs when rocks and other materials wear away the river channel.		

☞ Now, check your answers with a friend. Write the correct answer for those that are wrong. Your teacher will help you.

Geography Rivers: from source to sea © Folens (copiable page)

Activity sheet – River erosion

What is weathering?

The weather creates changes on the surfaces of things around us. For example, buildings may crumble and metal may rust as a result of weathering.

There are several kinds of weathering:

- physical weathering: when the wind, rain, sun or other kinds of weather break down rocks
- chemical weathering: when the acid in rainwater creates a chemical change
- biological weathering: when plants and animals break down materials.

☞ Study the pictures below with a partner and discuss what is happening in each. Then, working separately, write down what type of weathering is happening. Check your answers with your partner. Try to agree on your answers together.

....

Erosion and weathering

☞ Using what you have learnt, complete this writing frame.

We have been finding out about…

....

The river erodes…

....

One type of erosion is…

....

which means…

....

Another example is…

....

This means…

....

On the other hand, weathering…

....

because…

....

We can see examples of weathering when…

....

and also…

....

So the difference between erosion and weathering is that…

....

Teacher's notes

River transportation

Objectives

- Learn that the river transports materials through suspension, solution, saltation and traction
- Understand that river erosion and transportation work together

Prior knowledge

Students should be aware that a river changes from source to mouth and understand the different courses of the river. They should be able to read some polysyllabic words.

QCA links

Unit 7 Rivers – a fieldwork approach

NC links

Breadth of study 6 Themes c

Scottish attainment targets

Environmental Studies – Society – people and place
Strand – The physical environment
Level E, Level F

Environmental Studies – Science – Earth and space
Strand – Changing materials
Level C

Wales NC links

Themes 2 Rivers

Northern Ireland NC links

Rocks and processes of landscape development d
Fluvial

Background

The river transports material in a variety of ways as well as eroding it. How much erosion and transportation occur will depend on how much energy the river has, which in turn will depend on the gradient, how full the river is and the channel shape. A fast flowing river will erode and transport more quickly and easily. The material that the river erodes (its 'load') is also transported by it and the material transported helps the river to erode. Therefore, the two processes, erosion and transportation, work closely together. When the river lacks energy, however, it will deposit or drop its load.

Starter activity

Explore the types of things carried in rivers with students, asking them to name the lightest of objects and material, for example, feathers (lightest) and boulders (heaviest). Ask students to think about how each object would travel. Draw up examples on the board.

Resource and activity sheets

The two resource sheets, 'River transportation (1) and (2)' deal respectively with: solution and suspension and saltation and traction. Go through the different transportation processes with students, ensuring they grasp how each works and the keywords as needed. Then, use the activity sheet, 'Cause and effect'. Discuss what the two terms 'cause' and 'effect' mean by referring to the example given. Each student should complete the activity sheet on their own. The last statement (River transports materials) requires students to have grasped that material is transported because of the river's energy.

Use activity sheets, 'What could happen?' and 'What did happen?' to carry out a demonstration, which shows how different materials are carried (and deposited) in rivers. Show students a jar filled with sand, soil and gravel, or with river water and sediment taken, for example, during a field trip. The jar should be shaken and observed to see how different particles settle. Students should then assess which particles might be carried in different ways, depending on the force of the river. For example, what might be carried by suspension? Use the first of the two activity sheets, 'What could happen?' before the experiment and instruct students to make predictions. (They should draw on the work already carried out under 'River transportation (1) and (2)'). The final activity sheet, 'What did happen?' can be used to record the students' results.

Plenary

Ask students to discuss their results from the experiment above and use these to reinforce the different forms of river transportation where possible. If students are on a field trip, they can note how other materials (for example, twigs and leaves) are carried in the flow.

River transportation (1)

☞ Rivers transport the materials they erode downstream. They carry their load in several ways. Study the pictures below. Make sure you know the meanings of the keywords.

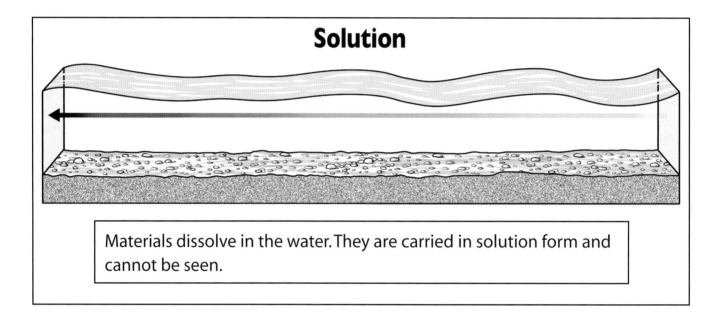

Solution

Materials dissolve in the water. They are carried in solution form and cannot be seen.

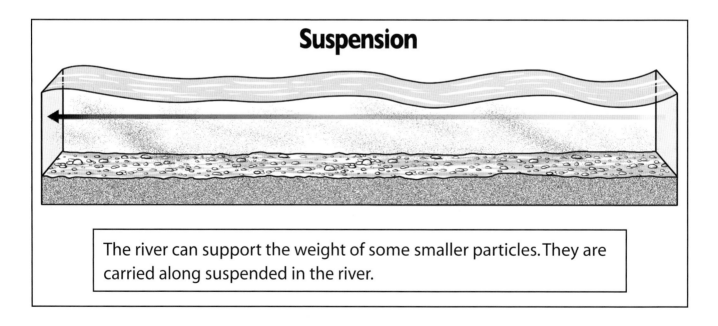

Suspension

The river can support the weight of some smaller particles. They are carried along suspended in the river.

Keywords

transportation   downstream   the river's load   solution   suspension

River transportation (2)

☞ Rivers transport the materials they erode downstream. They carry their load in several ways. Study the pictures below. Make sure you know the meanings of the keywords.

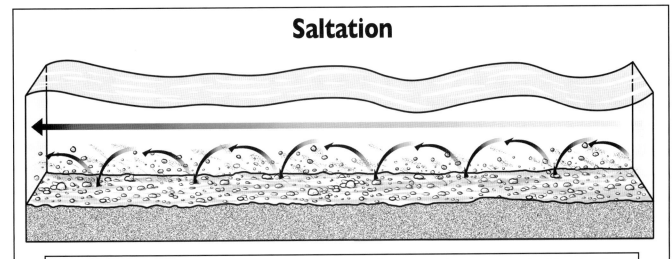

Saltation

Some stones and large sand grains are too heavy to be suspended in the fast-flowing water. Instead, they bounce along the riverbed.

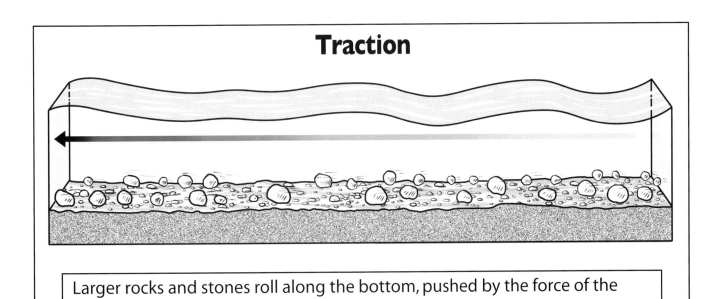

Traction

Larger rocks and stones roll along the bottom, pushed by the force of the water.

Keywords		
saltation	traction	riverbed

Cause and effect

Remember!
A CAUSE is the reason why something happens.
An EFFECT is the result of something happening.

☞ Look at this example.

Ravi's <u>clever footwork</u> meant he scored <u>a goal</u>.

reason (cause) of the goal   result (effect) of clever footwork

☞ Now, use the resource sheets, 'River transportation (1) and (2)', to help you to write down the missing causes in this table.

Cause	Effect
	Some materials are suspended in the river and are carried along.
	Some materials that are carried in the river can't be seen.
	Some rocks and stones roll along the riverbed.
	Some rocks and stones bounce along the riverbed.
	Rivers transports materials.

Activity sheet – River transportation

What could happen?

☞ Your teacher will provide you with a demonstration to show how different materials are carried (and deposited) in rivers. Complete the writing frame to show what you think could happen.

Name:
Demonstration to be carried out: Materials: Equipment: Method:
I expect to find that…   and that…   and also that…

Activity sheet – River transportation

What did happen?

☞ Now, complete these writing and drawing frames to show what did happen.

Name:
Demonstration carried out:

Draw pictures to show what happened:

I found out that…. (write a paragraph)

☞ Were your predictions correct? **Yes/No**

Teacher's notes

River deposition

Objectives

- Learn that the river deposits material
- Understand how an oxbow lake is formed
- Understand that the formation of an oxbow lake depends on deposition and erosion

Prior knowledge

Students should be aware that a river changes from source to mouth and understand the different courses of the river. They should be able to read some polysyllabic words.

QCA links

Unit 7 Rivers – a fieldwork approach

NC links

Breadth of study 6 Themes c

Scottish attainment targets

Environmental Studies – Society – people and place
Strand – The physical environment
Level E

Wales NC links

Themes 2 Rivers or Coasts

Northern Ireland NC links

Rocks and processes of landscape development d Fluvial

Background

Deposition occurs when the river has insufficient energy to carry its load. This happens in the middle and particularly the lower course of the river, for example, where the river has wide meanders. Material will be deposited on the inside bend of the meander (while erosion occurs on the outside, where the flow has greater energy). A river also deposits its load as it enters the sea, or a lake. At estuaries, which are tidal mouths, deposits of silt often build up creating mudflats. Deltas, also the result of large-scale deposition (where the river splits around the silt, creating channels), are often found at the mouths of large rivers such as the Ganges, the Nile and the Mississippi.

Starter activity

Refer students back to the unit on River transportation and the experiment to show how different materials respond in water and are carried along. (You may wish to demonstrate this again.) Then, use the experiment to discuss deposition, showing how as the water stills, the materials settle at the bottom of the jar at different rates.

Resource and activity sheets

The first resource sheet, 'Meandering rivers', shows a cross section of a river in the lowland regions as it travels across its flood plain. The meander is labelled to show how deposition and erosion occur. Go through the cross section with students, pointing out the labels and keywords: **meander, river beach, river cliff** and **flood plain**. Ensure students grasp that this process takes place over a long period of time. Follow, by asking students to complete the activity sheet, 'What is missing?'. This is a cloze exercise, which relates to the cross-section provided on the resource page, 'Meandering rivers'. Keywords are provided.

The next resource sheet, 'oxbow lakes' can be used to show students a formed oxbow lake. Students should move to the next activity sheet, 'An Oxbow Lake: how could one form?', to view illustrations, which show how an oxbow lake is formed. Go through the captions provided. Students should complete this activity sheet from memory. This sheet focuses on what could happen if a river floods.

Use the final activity sheet, 'River map', to see if students can identify the features covered in this unit on a simple map of a meandering river.

Plenary

Discuss the labels students have added to their meandering river maps, correcting them as necessary. They could have included the following: *river, meanders, inner bend of meander, outer bend of meander, oxbow lake, narrow neck of land, river beach, river cliff, sediment, flood plain.*

Meandering rivers

☞ As the river reaches the end of its course, it has less energy, so it becomes slower. It zig-zags in wide loops called meanders. Study this picture. Make sure you know the meanings of the keywords.

river cliff

meander

Here the river travels quickly and erodes the land, so that a river cliff may form.

river beach

Here the river travels slowly. It deposits material (sediment). This can build up to form a river beach.

Keywords

meander   river beach   river cliff   flood plain

Geography Rivers: from source to sea

© Folens (copiable page)

Activity sheet – River deposition

What is missing?

☞ The sentences below describe a river in its lower course. Finish the sentences by writing down the correct words in the spaces. Use the word bank to help you.

In the lowlands a river swings from side to side across its __ __ __ __ __ __ __ __ __ __ __ .
In this way, it can create large loops called __ __ __ __ __ __ __ __ . On the inside bend of the meander the river flows __ __ __ __ __ __ __ and cannot carry its __ __ __ __ , so it __ __ __ __ __ __ __ __ it.

On the outside of the meander's bend, the river is travelling __ __ __ __ __ __ , so, instead of dropping the material, it __ __ __ __ __ __ the landscape.

```
                        Word bank
        erodes       flood plain       deposits       quickly
        slowly       meanders          load
```

☞ Now, take it in turns to read your finished sentences to a partner. Do they agree?

Resource sheet – River deposition

Oxbow lakes

☞ Sometimes a meander can form a very wide loop. This means there may only be a narrow neck between the two ends of the loop. Over time the two sides can meet or the river may flood the land. Then an oxbow lake will form. Study the picture below.

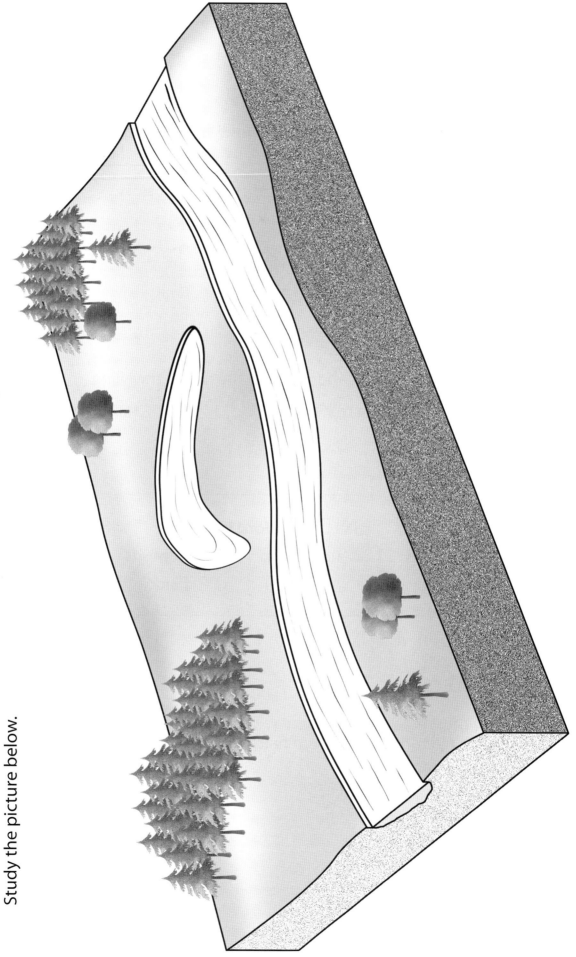

Geography Rivers: from source to sea

Activity sheet – River deposition

An oxbow lake: how could one form?

☞ The following statements describe how an oxbow lake could form. Write them in the correct order in the boxes under each picture.

- **The river shifts course and leaves behind an oxbow lake.**
- **The river has wide loops called meanders.**
- **The meander is cut off if the river floods.**
- **When the meanders get wider, the neck of land narrows.**

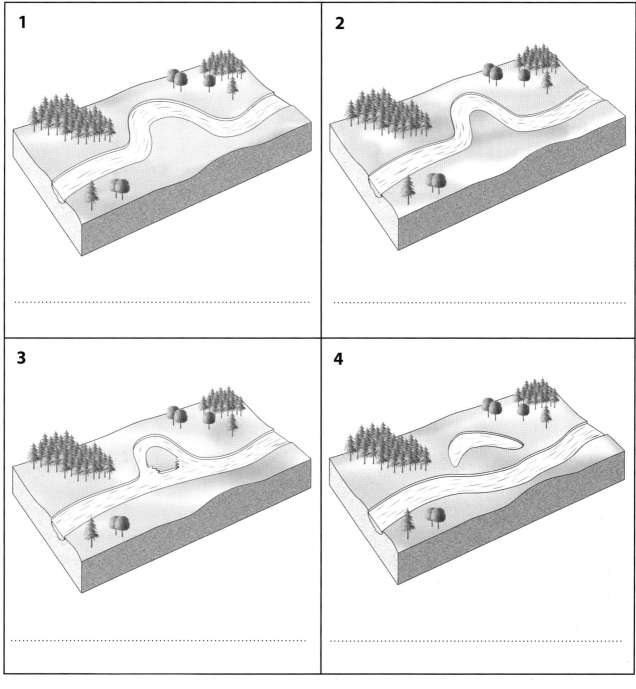

Activity sheet – River deposition

River map

☞ Study the map below. Label as many features of the river as you can. You should try to label at least eight!

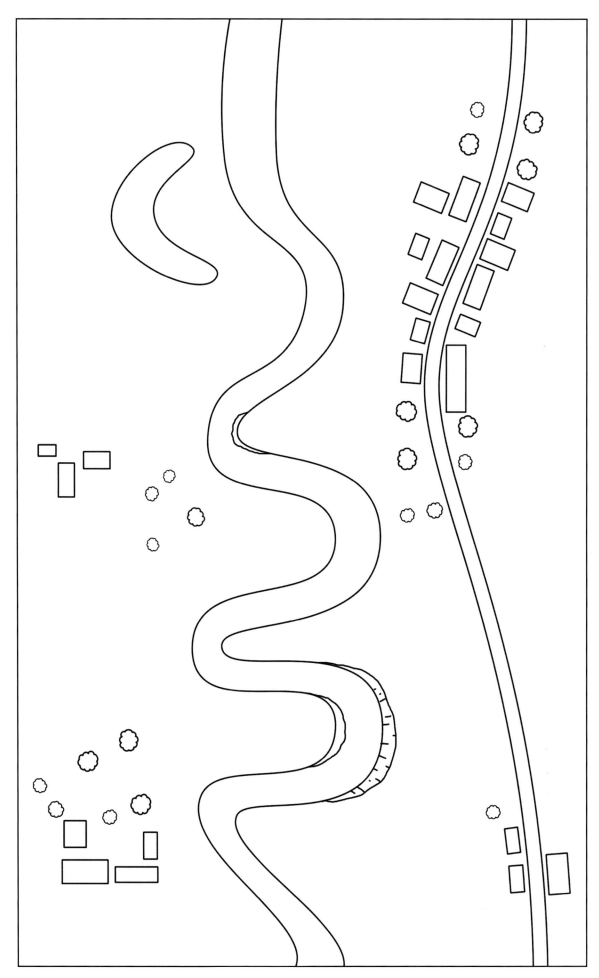

Geography Rivers: from source to sea
© Folens (copiable page)

Teacher's notes

River landscapes, drainage basins and river valleys

Objectives

- Understand what a drainage basin is
- Understand how a river valley is formed

Prior knowledge

Students should be aware of the different courses of the river and that rivers shape landscapes.

QCA links

Unit 7 Rivers – a fieldwork approach

NC links

Knowledge and understanding of places 3 a
Breadth of study 6 Themes c

Scottish attainment targets

Environmental Studies – Society – people and place
Strand – The physical environment
Level E – describe some obvious physical features and the processes that formed them.

Environmental Studies – Society – enquiry
Strand – Preparing for tasks
Level D
Strand – Carrying out tasks
Level D

Wales NC links

Themes 2 Rivers or Coasts

Northern Ireland NC links

Rocks and processes of landscape development d
Fluvial

Background

The area of land that slopes down towards the river and is drained by it (and any tributaries and streams it has) is called the drainage basin. The land between two drainage basins is called the watershed. Some drainage basins are gigantic. The River Amazon drains almost two fifths of the South American continent.

River valleys are shaped by the course of the river and have different features at different points. In the mountains where the river erodes downwards, deep into the land, a 'V' shape is formed, with little valley floor. Spurs of land develop as the river twists and turns around hard rock, while eroding downwards. Further downhill, where tributaries join and it is less steep, the river erodes sideways as well as downwards, widening its channel, until in the lower course the river meanders in wide loops. Here the channel floor is very wide and the valley sides can be hardly seen.

Starter activity

Carry out a brainstorming exercise and ask students to name features of the river's processes, reinforcing the keywords **erosion** and **deposition**. Students can record the feature, along with its process or processes, for example, a river beach or a river cliff.

Resource and activity sheets

The resource sheets, 'River valley' and 'Drainage basins' can be used together. Take students through the features of the river valley first, before discussing resource sheet, 'Drainage basins'. (See **Background** for discussion points.)

Waterfalls are often found in the upper course of a river (though they may occur elsewhere). There are many kinds, but typically a waterfall is formed as the river meets hard then soft rock, the latter eroding more quickly, leaving the former jutting out as a ledge, over which the water spills. (This ledge will in time fall and the waterfall will shift backwards.) Go through the formation of a waterfall with students instructing them to complete the activity sheet, 'How does a waterfall form?' As well as using the keywords **hard rock** and **plunge pool**, students could add the following labels: 'ledge', 'river', and 'waterfall', to the diagram and complete the captions: 'soft rock erodes quickly', 'hard rock erodes slowly', 'the plunge pool is eroded by fallen rocks and water'.

Once students have grasped the shape of the changing valley and some of its physical features, ask them to complete the activity sheet, 'The changing valley' on their own using what they have learnt to help them. They should identify which sentences belong to which parts of the valley. The final activity sheet 'Great rivers', depicts many of the world's largest rivers in their different continents. Students can work in pairs (and under guidance use ICT) to complete a database of information about each river. Before they begin refer students to the size of some of the drainage basins and their features. See **Background** for more information.

Plenary

Recap the keywords used in this unit by asking students to work in pairs to share the information they found for their databases.

River valley

Study this river valley as it changes with the journey of the river, from source to mouth.

'V'shaped valley

river erodes downward

river erodes sideways and downward

waterfall

interlocking spurs

tributaries

river widens valley floor

Geography Rivers: from source to sea

Resource sheet – River landscapes, drainage basins and river valleys

Drainage basins

☞ Water from higher ground drains into a river and its tributaries. The water will come from gentler slopes as well as mountains. From the air, a pattern is formed that looks like a tree with many branches. This is the drainage basin. The land between two **drainage basins** is called a **watershed**. This might be a mountain, hill or a ridge. Study this drainage basin.

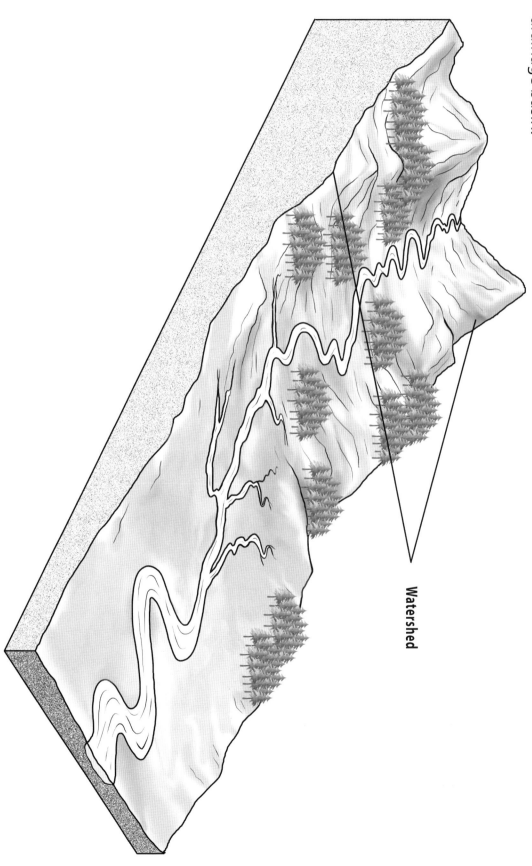

Watershed

How does a waterfall form?

☞ Make sure you understand how a waterfall forms. Your teacher will help you. Then, label the diagram below with these words:

- **hard rock**
- **plunge pool**

☞ Some other labels are missing. Think of three more words and add them to the diagram.

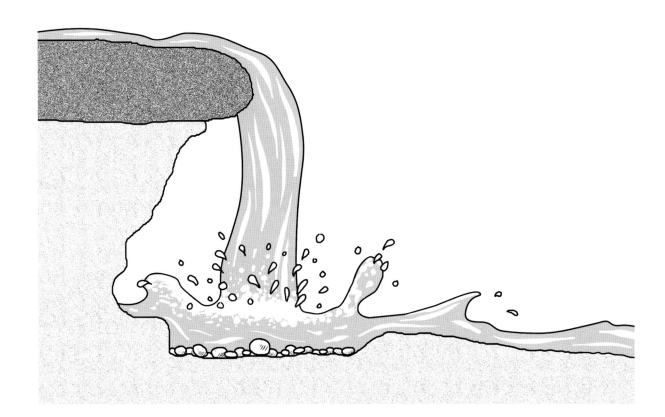

☞ Now, finish these captions and add them to the correct places on the diagram.

Soft rock erodes __ __ __ __ __ __ __ .

Hard rock erodes __ __ __ __ __ __ __ .

The plunge pool is eroded by __ __ __ __ __ __   __ __ __ __ __ and __ __ __ __ __ .

Activity sheet – River landscapes, drainage basins and river valleys

The changing valley

☞ In which of the three boxes below do each of these sentences belong? Write the numbers down. Remember some boxes will have more than one number.

1 Spurs jut out.

2 Waterfalls are often found here.

3 The river erodes sideways as well as downward.

4 A deep 'V' shaped valley is formed.

5 The valley sides can hardly be seen.

Highland valley

Valley where it is less steep

Lowland valley

☞ Now, write a paragraph to sum up how the valley changes from highland to lowland.

....

....

....

Activity sheet – River landscapes, drainage basins and river valleys

Great rivers

☞ Below are some of the longest rivers in the world with huge drainage basins. Work with a partner and carry out research for each river. Include the following keywords:

- length of river
- source
- area of drainage basin
- mouth
- tributaries

☞ What else could you include? Find out two more facts about each river.

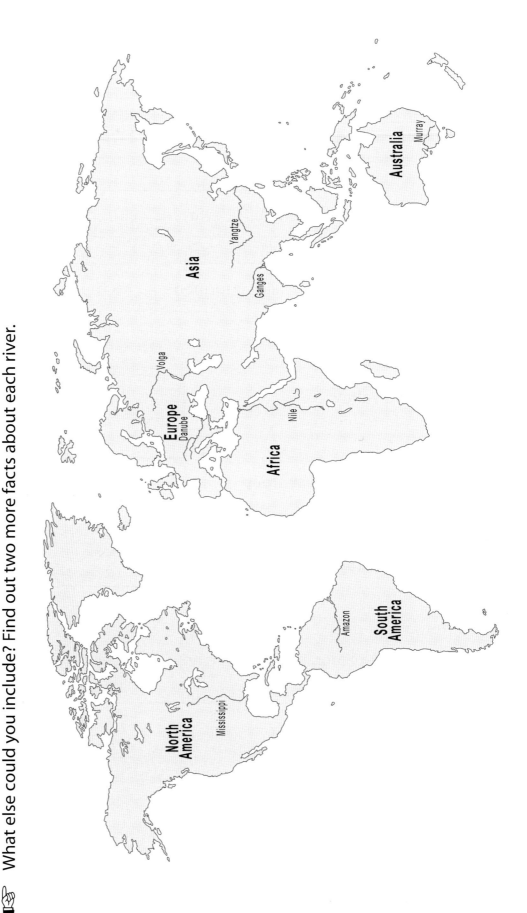

Geography Rivers: from source to sea

© Folens (copiable page)

Teacher's notes

Flooding

Objectives

- Understand the effects of floods
- Understand how communities respond to floods
- Learn the causes of floods in Bangladesh and that floods can have benefits

Prior knowledge

Students should be aware of localities beyond their own, and of natural disasters in different part of the world.

QCA links

Unit 4 Flood disaster – how do people cope?

NC links

Breadth of study 6 Themes c ii
Knowledge and understanding of places 3 a

Scottish attainment targets

Environmental Studies – Society – people and place
Strand – The physical environment
Level D, Level F

Wales NC links

Themes 2 Rivers or Coasts

Northern Ireland NC links

Weather and climate f

Background

In 2004, in the Cornish village of Boscastle, two rivers burst their banks and deluged the village. An immense amount of damage occurred. (Flash floods happen when there is heavy rainfall over a short period of time. The water cannot infiltrate the ground quickly enough and runs off.) Flooding is, however, a normal part of a river's processes and floods can be beneficial. For example, it can enrich the soil with silt, as happens in Bangladesh (though climate change and sea-level rise are likely to threaten much of this area in the future). Another example is the Nile, which was central to Egypt's growth. Before the building of the Aswan Dam, heavy rains caused the Nile to overflow. The silt left behind meant that farming was possible in a desert region. Crops, fish and wildlife flourished, producing a plentiful supply of food.

Starter activity

Under supervision, ask students to work in pairs to carry out a quick Internet search (for example on the BBC weather website) to identify recent floods in Britain. They could research the Boscastle disaster in particular (as highlighted in **Background**). Ask them to share their findings and describe how they would feel (or have felt) in such circumstances.

Resource and activity sheets

Students could work in pairs to identify the numbered features on the resource page, 'Overflowing rivers', which they should then use to record on the spider diagram provided on the next sheet. Encourage them to ask questions such as: *What parts are badly damaged? What parts are unaffected? What are the emergency services doing?* If students are working together, they should each complete the spider diagram on the activity sheet, 'What is happening?', which they will need for reference when completing activity sheet, 'Flood report'. A writing frame has been provided to help students to structure the report, but as far as possible students should write the report on their own.

Teachers may need to read the resource sheet, 'Bangladesh', to students, but encourage them to join in where they can. Draw out the keyword: **monsoon**, and focus on the two contrasting images presented; a country that suffers devastating floods but also one that is, at present, rich in fertile land, necessary to feed the population. This sheet also discusses the causes of floods. Students should complete the accompanying activity sheet, 'Disasters and benefits', which looks at the causes and effects of flooding, when they have grasped all the points discussed on the former sheet.

Plenary

Ask students to report back on the work done under, 'Disasters and benefits'. Ensure they understand the relationship between cause and effect, for example, heavy rain or soil erosion and build-up in rivers can cause floods, and also any further effects, such as silt provides rich soil, which leads to farming.

Resource sheet – Flooding

Overflowing rivers

☞ Study this picture of a flooded town. Then, complete the activity sheet, 'What is happening?'

Geography Rivers: from source to sea

Activity sheet – Flooding

What is happening?

☞ Study the picture of the floods on the resource sheet, 'Overflowing rivers'. Decide what each number tells you.

Now, record what you can see on the spider diagram. The first one has been done for you.

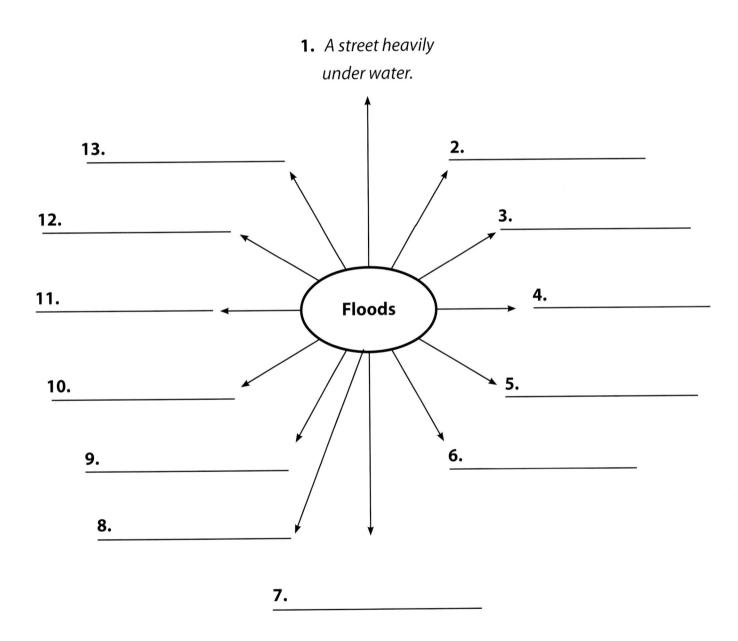

1. *A street heavily under water.*

13. _____

12. _____

11. _____

10. _____

9. _____

8. _____

7. _____

2. _____

3. _____

4. _____

5. _____

6. _____

Floods

☞ On your spider diagram, circle all the examples of flood damage.

Activity sheet – Flooding

Flood report

 Imagine you are a BBC reporter. You have been sent to the scene of some floods. Write the report you will send in to the BBC website. Write three paragraphs in the writing frame below. Include these topics:

- **How many rivers were involved?**
- **Flood damage**
- **The rescue worker's role**

NEWS

Date: Reporter:

Reporting from:

Paragraph 1

Today the small town of……..

Paragraph 2

Paragraph 3

Resource sheet – Flooding

Bangladesh

☞ Read the following:

In some parts of the world floods can cause deaths and much damage. Most of Bangladesh in Asia is situated on low-lying land. Several great rivers meet there. These are the rivers Ganges, Bramaphutra and Meghna, which flow into the Bay of Bengal. Each river also has other rivers (tributaries) running into it.

In the monsoon season very heavy rainfall causes terrible floods. Thousands can die and homes and crops are swept away. In some areas there is also serious river erosion. Soil is washed into the rivers. This means the rivers can hold less water so they flood more easily.

Why do people live here? There are many reasons. One reason is that when the rivers flood, they leave behind silt. This is very rich soil, which is good for farming. Vital crops such as rice and wheat are grown here. The silt also means there is a good supply of fish.

So, in Bangladesh floods can bring disaster, but also benefits.

Activity sheet – Flooding

Disasters and benefits

☞ You will need to use the resource page, 'Bangladesh' to complete these activities.

- Find all the names of rivers or places mentioned. Now, find these on an atlas or globe.

Underline in red: (If you need to underline the same part twice, underline again in black.)
- when the rivers flood
- the damage caused by floods
- two causes of flooding.

☞ Now, fill in this table to show the causes of flooding.

Cause	Effect
A	flooding
B	flooding

☞ Still using the resource sheet, 'Bangladesh', underline in blue the reason why silt occurs. Then underline what silt helps to create.

☞ Now, fill in this table.

Cause	Effect	Effect
	silt ⟶	1.
		2.

Geography Rivers: from source to sea   © Folens (copiable page)

Teacher's notes

Floods: causes and control

Objectives

- Identify some reasons why rivers flood and look at a case study
- Learn about different kinds of flood defences
- Understand that some flood defences can create problems

Prior knowledge

Students should be aware of localities beyond their own and of natural disasters through the television and other media.

QCA links

Unit 4 Flood disaster – how do people cope?

NC links

Breadth of study 6 Themes cii

Scottish attainment targets

Environmental Studies – Society – people and place
Strand – The physical environment
Level D, Level E

Environmental Studies – Society – developing informed attitudes
Strand – Social and environmental responsibility
Level D, E

Wales NC links

Themes 2 Rivers or Coasts

Northern Ireland NC links

Weather and climate f

Background

While flooding is part of the river's process, floods can occur as a result of human intervention. For example, deepening and straightening the Mississippi to increase its flow and make it easier for river traffic can create flooding downstream; built up areas cannot absorb water; deforestation means less transpiration and fewer trees may also allow soil to be washed into rivers, blocking them. Flood control measures largely fall into soft engineering (terraces, reforestation, renewing wetlands) and hard engineering (concrete levees, dams, barriers).

Starter activity

Recap on the work covered in the unit on 'Flooding', which looks at the devastation caused by floods,

how local communities cope, the cause of floods in Bangladesh and the benefits.

Resource and activity sheets

The resource sheet, 'Rivers and their floodplains', depicts several situations where floods can occur. Students should describe what could happen in each example if the river flooded. Remind students of transpiration and the role of vegetation in the water cycle. Emphasise that hard surfaces do not absorb water. Ask students: *where would the water go?*

'Case study: the River Lee' provides students with a case study which they should use to complete the fact file which follows. The fact file comprises six facts which the children should pick out and write down in the space provided. Facts which students should note down include: *two rivers (for example, the Ash and Stort) flow into the River Lee; the River Lee often floods; the 1947 winter was very cold; the English Channel partly froze ; rain began falling in mid-March.* Students can refer back to these when they complete the sequence of events that caused the River Lee to flood on activity sheet, 'Why did the River Lee flood?', which could be completed as follows: *In1947 very cold winter and thick snow until March ⟶ Rain in March caused snow to melt ⟶ This water (run-off) flowed at a high rate into Lee's tributaries and water rose ⟶ So water in River Lee rose rapidly above flood defences ⟶ Severe floods.*

The activity sheet, 'Soft and hard flood defences' focuses on hard and soft engineering. Introduce the key defences and go through the illustrations provided about each. Draw out that flood defences can unwittingly create flooding elsewhere (see **Background** for more detail). Point out that increasingly, flood management favours soft engineering. Students should then group each example given under the correct heading: 'Hard engineering' or 'Soft engineering'. The final activity sheet, 'Key points', asks students to identify the main points which have been covered in this unit and to give examples.

Plenary

Discuss with students the key points they have made on the final activity sheet. Then Refer back to the 'Case study: the River Lee' and ask them to identify three related causes for the floods, for example: frozen ground meant snow lay thick; rainfall caused melting and high rate of run-off; water levels rose rapidly in Lee's tributaries.

Resource sheet – Floods: causes and control

Rivers and their floodplains

In heavy rain, it is natural for rivers to flood. This is especially true where they flow across their floodplains. Towns and cities are often built on floodplains, so floods become a problem. Hard surfaces, such as roads, cannot absorb the water.

☞ Study the pictures below, which show places where floods can happen.

Geography Rivers: from source to sea

© Folens (copiable page)

Activity sheet – Floods: Causes and control

Case study: the River Lee

☞ Read this case study about the flooding of the River Lee.

The River Lee begins in the Chiltern Hills and flows south. On its way, other rivers, such as the Ash and the Stort, two of its tributaries, join it and it passes through many towns and districts.

The Lee is a river that often floods. In 1947, the winter had been very cold. Even the sea along the coast of the English Channel partly froze. The snow was still thick on the frozen ground until rain began to fall in mid-March. This caused the snow to melt rapidly. In turn, the water (called run-off) began to flow at a high rate into the rivers. These rivers ran into the River Lee.

Even though the River Lee had flood defences, the water rose so fast that the Lee burst its banks. Further heavy rain a few days later meant more flooding. It was not until a week had passed before the water levels were normal. During that time, millions of tonnes of extra water had passed into the River Lee.

☞ Now, in the case study, underline names of places, dates and other factual information you can find. Then, complete the fact file. The first one has been done by you.

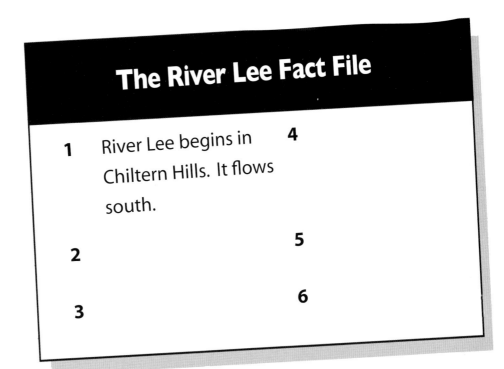

The River Lee Fact File

1 River Lee begins in Chiltern Hills. It flows south.

2

3

4

5

6

Activity Sheet – Floods: Causes and control

Why did the River Lee flood?

☞ You will need a copy of 'Case Study: the River Lee' and your fact file.

What were the sequence of events that caused the River Lee to flood? Write notes in the boxes below to explain. It has been started for you.

In 1947…

Geography Rivers: from source to sea © Folens (copiable page)

Soft and hard flood defences

Many flood defences have a major effect on the environment. They are also expensive. Soft engineering has less effect and is cheaper.

☞ Study the defences below. Which are 'hard engineering', and which are 'soft engineering'?

Dam
The dam holds back the river. The area behind the dam floods and creates a lake. Water flow is controlled by sluice gates.

Dredging and embankments
Removing large amounts of silt from the river to lower it and building banks with the silt.

Channels
These take the river in a new direction. They can have concrete beds and banks or earth ones.

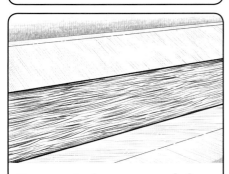

Concrete levees or dykes
These are built alongside rivers to keep them in their course.

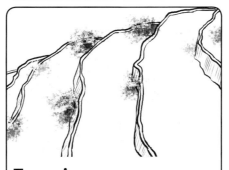

Terracing
Steps in the hillside make the land level and rainwater can be collected.

Reforestation
Planting trees, which take in water.

☞ Which of the defences are more environmently friendly? Why?

Follow up... Answer these questions on a separate piece of paper.

- Under your teacher's guidance use the Internet to find out about the Thames Flood barrier. How does it work? When is it used? Is it soft or hard engineering?

- What are sluice gates? How do they work?

- What happened to the levees in New Orleans in 2005?

Activity sheet – Floods: Causes and control

Key points

☞ Use what you have learnt to add some key points about flooding to the boxes below.

Topic: *Floods: causes and control*
Floods: Some causes   ....
Examples of flood defences   ....
Problems with flood defences   ....
What types of flood defences will be used in the future?   ....
Why?   ....

Teacher's notes

River pollution

Objectives

- Learn the causes and effects of river pollution
- Look at a case study and discuss, expressing and sharing opinions

Prior knowledge

Students should be aware of the term **'river pollution'** and have some knowledge of rivers and their processes. It will also be useful if students have experienced a river field trip.

QCA links

Unit 7 Rivers – a fieldwork approach

NC links

Knowledge and understanding of environmental change and sustainable development 5a
Breadth of study 7 Themes c

Scottish attainment targets

Environmental Studies – Society – people and place
Strand – Human – physical interactions
Level F

Environmental Studies – Society – developing informed attitudes
Strand – Social and environmental responsibility
Level E

Environmental Studies – Science – Earth and space
Strand – Changing materials
Level B
Strand – Materials from Earth
Level B

Wales NC links

Themes 8 Environmental issues

Northern Ireland NC links

Economic activities c

Background

Although there have been serious attempts to deal with river pollution and progress has been made, many rivers are still moderately or seriously polluted. Industry, agriculture and urbanisation are the main sources of pollution and accidents. Negligence or even deliberate flouting of the law can result in the wholesale destruction of, for example, fish stocks that have taken years to build up. Thermal pollution (changes, which occur when water, often from power plants, is discharged at a higher temperature into the river) affects the oxygen supply. This results in declining organisms or the overgrowth of others, such as algae, and the destruction of ecosystems.

Starter activity

Carry out a brainstorming exercise and ask students to name examples of pollution under the headings: **air**, **land**, **water** and **noise**.

Resource and activity sheets

You will need to discuss the resource sheet, 'Dirty waters' with students, ensuring they understand the different kinds of pollution and what is largely responsible for them. Refer to the **Background** information to explain keywords such as **acid rain**. If possible, students should visit a river (or canal) and assess the state of it. They can make observations, noting what life exists there, for example, mayfly nymphs usually indicate clean water; bloodworms indicate some pollution; algae, noxious smells and little life indicate heavy pollution. The activity sheet, 'Water quality' can then be used to record these details.

The second resource sheet, 'Case study: the river Ely', recounts the effects of a chlorine discharge into the Ely. The accompanying activity sheet, 'The River Ely: looking more closely', asks students to record details from the case study and to look at cause and effect. Students should then carry out research using the Internet (with your guidance) or the library to find out about other pollution incidents. They should record these facts in a fact file.

Ask students to use what they have learnt in this unit, by completing the writing frame on the activity sheet, 'River pollution summary'.

Plenary

Ask students to report back, and give information on their findings. Students can discuss, as a class, which were the worst cases and which, if detailed, had good outcomes.

Dirty waters

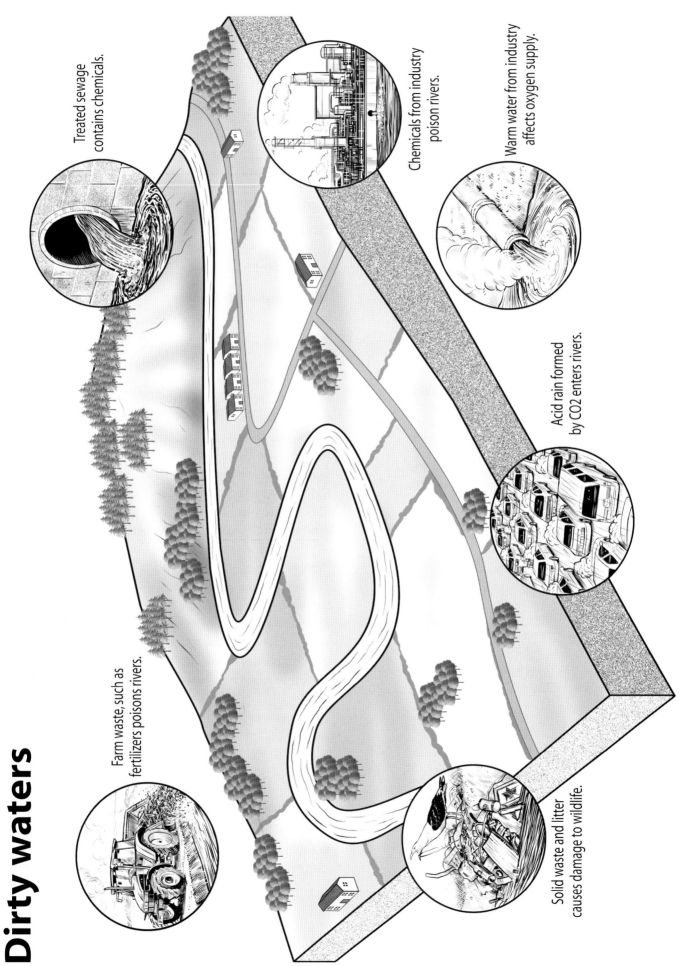

Treated sewage contains chemicals.

Chemicals from industry poison rivers.

Warm water from industry affects oxygen supply.

Acid rain formed by CO2 enters rivers.

Farm waste, such as fertilizers poisons rivers.

Solid waste and litter causes damage to wildlife.

Activity sheet – River pollution

Water quality

Observations of: _____   **Date:** _____

Equipment: _____

_____

☞ In the boxes below make drawings or diagrams to show what you did or saw and label them. Then write some sentences under each drawing to explain what you found out. Use more than one sheet if you need to.

Resource sheet – River pollution

Case study: the River Ely

☞ Read this case study.

The River Ely is an important Welsh river. Its source, along with the River Taff's, is in the Welsh mountains. From there the rivers flow south ending at Cardiff Bay. Both rivers were badly polluted in the 19th and 20th centuries. This was mainly due to the coal, iron and steel industries. As these industries declined, so the rivers became cleaner. Pollution control and a desire to create healthy rivers also made a difference. Water quality improved. Wildlife returned.

In 2005, however, the Ely received a setback – a stark reminder of how easily pollution can damage a healthy river. According to local people, fish were first seen dead and dying in May. This was over a two-mile stretch. The sighting was reported to the Environment Agency and tests were carried out. Chlorine, which is much the same as household bleach, had found its way into the river. Thousands of fish, including salmon and trout were lost.

This is not the first time the Ely has been damaged in recent years. Other British rivers including the nearby River Ebbw have also been polluted. Farm waste as well as industrial waste is often the cause.

Activity sheet – River pollution

The River Ely: looking more closely

☞ You will need to use the resource page, 'Case study: the River Ely' to help you to complete these activities:

- First read the headings and questions below.
- Then, find the information in the case study and underline it.
- Give answers under each of the headings.

Details:

Where is the River Ely?

_____

What is its history?

_____

_____

Pollution incident

When did this happen?

_____

_____

_____

What happened?

_____

_____

_____

What caused the pollution?

_____

_____

_____

River pollution summary

☞ Use what you have learnt to complete this writing frame.

I have been studying….

....

I found out that….

....

For example…

....

and…

....

and also…

....

In particular I did not know that…

....

and I felt that…

....

because…

....

One of the things I would like to find out more about is…

....

Teacher's notes

River conservation and renewal

Objectives

- Understand the term **conservation**.
- Look at a river renewal case study.

Prior knowledge

It will be useful if students have completed unit 9 'River pollution'. They should also have some knowledge of the river's course and its processes.

QCA links

Unit 7 Rivers – a fieldwork approach

NC links

Knowledge and understanding of environmental change and sustainable development

Scottish attainment targets

Environmental Studies – Society – people and place
Strand – Human – physical interactions
Level E

Environmental Studies – Society – developing informed attitudes
Strand – Social and environmental responsibility
Level E

Wales NC links

Themes 8 Environmental issues

Northern Ireland NC links

Places and locational knowledge: Issues: environmental

Background

The rescue of rivers and waterways from being straightened, channelled and controlled is becoming increasingly popular. There is a wider recognition in the UK and Europe that hard engineering projects not only damage the natural environment and are costly, but produce unintended effects. For example, shortening and deepening a river's channel to increase its speed can encourage erosion, so that the river dumps silt downstream. If flooding occurs, the river will find its own course again. Working with a river and its natural environment is preferable. Although it takes time for an ecosystem to develop, a river will nonetheless renew itself if it is cleaned and its natural surroundings encouraged. Management plans that are based on conservation and renewal, involving for example, limited building projects and planting suitable vegetation (rather than any vegetation) recognises that a river is a dynamic habitat.

Starter activity

Ask students what they understand the keyword, **conservation**, to mean. Ensure they grasp that it means the **renewal and management** of the Earth's natural resources as well as its **protection**. Introduce the keyword **biodiversity** as a central idea in conservation if you think suitable, and explain it simply as: *the number and variety of animals, plants and other organisms within a region.*

Resource and activity sheets

Read the resource sheets, 'Restoring a river (1) and (2)' to students, encouraging them to read where they can. Clarify any words students do not understand. The text traces the typical features of restoration: a river that has been extensively altered because of the danger of floods in urban areas; its decline; the involvement of pressure groups; the introduction of non-native species with disastrous results; the need to manage the river sensitively. After they have understood this, students should work in pairs to discuss and complete the tasks on the activity sheet, 'The Los Angeles River'.

Students should study in pairs each paragraph from the resource sheet, 'The Los Angeles River', to help them to answer the questions provided. Ask students to discuss their answers and to make notes in their work books. A map of the San Fernando Valley can be accessed via the Internet, under guidance when answering questions under the heading: **From source to sea**.

The final activity sheet, 'River file', can be used for students to research and record information about their local river and its health.

Plenary

In pairs, ask students to report back to other pairs, and explain their answers from the activity sheet, 'The Los Angeles River'.

Restoring a river (1)

From source to sea

Northwest of central Los Angeles lies the San Fernando Valley, which is bordered by mountain ranges. The Los Angeles River probably found its source from an underground river in the Simi Hills. The river flows east across the valley, then southeast near the Hollywood Hills, then south. Its mouth is at San Pedro Bay.

The 'concrete' river

The river is prone to drought and also floods. Since it flows through cities and industrial areas it has been deepened, channelled and straightened to try to prevent flooding. Much of the river's bed and sides have been lined with concrete. This has badly affected wildlife. It has also attracted graffiti and waste, and has become an eyesore over many years.

The Los Angeles River.

Geography Rivers: from source to sea

Restoring a river (2)

Master Plan

After continual pressure from conservation groups, something is to be done. In 2005 a 'Master Plan' was set up to try to renew the river. The plan includes cleaning the river and creating new habitats. The City of Los Angeles will oversee it and the general public will be asked to get involved. The whole plan will run over a period of twenty years.

Giant grasses

Where the river is not concreted, reeds and grasses grow. These are common to the area. There is also willow, ash, alder and other native trees, which allow bird species to thrive. A serious problem, however, is Arundo, a type of giant grass introduced into the California region. The native plants become swamped by it and few animals can exist along the banks. Some of the lowland rivers are seriously invaded. Attempts are being made to ensure the Los Angeles River does not go the same way.

Looking after wildlife

One development may be a wildlife corridor. It could travel along much of the river through the San Fernando Valley to San Pedro Bay. This would mean that nature could survive better where the river is concreted. At present, local people and conservation groups check the effects of pollution on the river and its wildlife. A range of sites is monitored. Students from the region's schools also undertake projects focusing on the river and its habitat. Such projects encourage a concern for nature, which can become a life-long interest.

What the Los Angeles River might become.

Activity sheet – River conservation and renewal

The Los Angeles River

☞ Use the resource sheets, 'Restoring a river (1) and (2)' to help you to answer these questions.

Work with a partner. Study each of the questions below and answer them in your work books.

From source to sea

1. Underline the words, which tell you the direction that the river takes. Then, find the river on a map showing California. Your teacher will help you.

2. What other important river seems to run parallel with it?

The 'concrete' river

3. The river has been 'deepened channelled and straightened'. What does this mean? Why has it happened?

4. What has altering the river done?

Master Plan

5. What is the Master Plan and how long will it run?

6. Why do you think the plan has come about?

7. Who will be involved? Why is this sensible?

Looking after wildlife

8. Why do you think the wildlife needs a 'corridor'?

9. What are conservation groups? What do they do?

10. Who do conservation groups work with in this case? Why is this useful? (Think of more than one reason).

Giant grasses

11. What native plants grow by the river? Why are they important?

12. Discuss the **cause** and **effect** of 'Arundo'.

River file

☞ Complete this fact file about your local river.

Name:	Date:

My local river:
Its source:
Its mouth:
Some places it travels through:
Tributaries, if any:
Managed by:
Water quality:
Examples of wildlife in and around the river:
Any improvements (in the last few years) and on-going improvements:
Conservation plans for the river:
Are there any other plans? If so, how will this affect the river environment?
Opportunities for the public to get involved in conservation work:

Assessment sheet

Tick the boxes to show what you know or what you can do.

	no / yes	not sure / sometimes	don't know / no
1. I listen to the teacher			
2. I work well with a partner			
3. I can work well in a group			
4.			
5.			
6.			
7.			
8.			
9.			
10.			

I know best / I can do best:

....

....

I need to: (Write no more than three targets.)

....

....

....